How to *Win* Students and *Inspire* Them

The Only Book You Need to Transform Your Classroom

Dr. Courtney L. Teague

How To Win Students And Inspire Them: Transforming Your Classroom

This book is dedicated to my mother Linda T. Caldwell.

Thank you for pushing and praying for me.
Your talks were not in vain.

Contents

Preface

This book is intended to be read with pencil in hand. Think of this as a workbook for self-study and professional development. The exercises contained herein are meant to facilitate your development as a teacher. You can use this book by yourself, with a colleague, or as the basis for a series of professional development workshops.

This book may well change your life as a teacher. While we all ask key existential questions at times, there is no more basic, fundamental, or critical query than, "Why do I teach?" To answer this question is to face a great mystery in your life. If you are willing to step out in faith and take the risk of exploring this mystery, then this book is for you!

When you ask yourself the question, "Why do I teach?" you embark upon a journey of personal and professional growth. The journey will be difficult, yet rewarding. In the following pages, you will be asked some rather tough questions. If you wish to fully benefit from this book, you will persevere with them, working through each question until it is fully answered. You will come out on the other end of this experience much more fully equipped to enter the classroom each day. Your desire to teach will be stoked, turning it into a burning passion to inspire your students.

Will you commit to completing the exercises thoroughly and honestly? If you take your personal and professional development seriously, you may well discover things about yourself that will lead to significant changes in your life—and in the lives of your students.

Are you willing to change? Many teachers have been moved to adopt practices that inspire their students after completing just one or two of these exercises. While you can read this book through in about an hour, the impact from completing the accompanying exercises may last a lifetime.

If you are ready to face yourself, read on! You will not be disappointed.

—Dr. Courtney L. Teague

Introduction

Do you remember when you used to draw birds that looked like checkmarks and a sun that looked like a half-eaten Oreo cookie? I bet you couldn't wait to share your drawings with your family and see them magnetted to the front of the refrigerator!

Do you remember your immense feeling of satisfaction as you explained what you had drawn while the other person just nodded, agreeing with your beautiful work of art? These feelings of satisfaction, affirmation, accomplishment, and a job well done are part of what I'm sure you wish for your learners, as well.

Oh, and by the way, when I talk about "students" and "learners" I'm talking about the same thing: the people who are the focus of your attention as a teacher. The same thing goes for the terms "teacher" and "educator."

Look Back

While we're thinking of your past, do you remember your favorite classroom teachers? What strategies did they employ that made you feel this way? I'd be willing to bet you've absorbed some of these tactics into the way you teach today.

What about the teachers who should have never become teachers? Do you remember why you thought that way? How did they make you feel? Can you identify specific things they did that engendered those feelings?

Everything I just asked you is part of my purpose for writing this book. I want to help you serve as a reflective change agent, a teacher who is able win students and inspire them.

Time for Personal Reflection

If you haven't already, take some time to think through your life and answer the questions I've already posed to you. I highly recommend you write down your thoughts so you can refer to them later.

Here's one more question for you to mull over before we move on. Why would anyone want to learn from you? Hmmm?

Now that you've courageously tackled these questions, let's hone in on the purpose behind them.

Your Strengths

As a teacher, have you ever taken inventory of your personal strengths? Really. There is a reason why you have the title teacher, and it isn't because you hold a degree or have passed a state test. Trust me. You have a group of personal strengths that have contributed to bringing you to your current level of success as a teacher.

Now is not the time for false humility. Try to remember any positive statements you have heard from others about your teaching. It is time to face some facts about yourself and your future as a teacher. Now is the time to reflect on your positive thinking, your motivation, planning, organization, active communication, listening and decision-making strengths. Before we go on, take a moment to write down what you, and others, have identified as personal strengths.

So, how did it go? Was it easy to write out your strengths, or did you find it difficult to identify even a few? If you found it hard to remember a time someone praised you for a personal strength, don't be surprised. The fact that we have difficulty remembering good things others say about us exposes a weakness in our profession. We, as a teaching community, seldom acknowledge the good we see in each other. I hope we, as teachers, will begin to change that.

Why Should I Care?

You may think that all this personal evaluation stuff is totally irrelevant to inspiring your students, but you couldn't be more mistaken. Your understanding of yourself affects every aspect of your teaching and plays a major role in your effectiveness as a world-changing teacher. And you are a world-changer! Don't forget for a moment that your influence is shaping the lives of individuals who will, in time, shape the world in which we all live.

It's important that you approach your classroom with confidence. And I'm not talking about bravado or proud self- importance. I mean a calm awareness of your abilities, your personality strengths, and your acquired skills. Live and work from these, and you will do well.

Of course, you have your weaknesses, too, but your strengths should be your focus. If you approach your day with fear, you can be sure that your students will pick up on it. It probably resonates with their own fears! Instead, approach your work with all the confidence that your lifetime of preparation has given you. Your students will more readily learn from you if they sense you are approaching things from a standpoint of confidence.

Ultimately, the way you feel about yourself will be reflected in the way you treat both students and peers. You know your reptilian brain can't tell the difference between self-love and love of others. Therefore, it is all the more important to have a calm, realistic understanding of who you are and what are your capabilities. This lays the groundwork for you to influence others for good.

This applies not only to your curriculum-related work with your students, but also to your interactions on a personal level. I am sure that if we as teachers were as supportive of our students, personally, as we want to be regarding their academics, there would be no need for extra programs to promote their emotional well-being.

Life's Work Assignment

Before we go any deeper into ways you can inspire your students, I want you to write down ten strengths you have as a world-changing teacher.

1.____________________________________
2.____________________________________
3.____________________________________
4.____________________________________
5.____________________________________
6.____________________________________
7.____________________________________
8.____________________________________
9.____________________________________
10.___________________________________

By building on these strengths, you can become even more effective as a teacher and inspire even more students.

Ralph Waldo Emerson said, "Our chief want is someone who will inspire us to be what we know we could be." Former CBS News anchor Dan Rather affirmed Emerson when he said, "The dream begins with a teacher who believes in you, who tugs and pushes and leads you to the next plateau, sometimes poking you with a sharp stick called truth."

How To Benefit From This Book

Here are nine suggestions to get the most out of this book:

1. Know why you are reading this book. Only read this book if you want to learn how to increase the influence you have on your students. You may ask, "How can I increase my desire to learn?" Well, the answer is simple. All you need to do is constantly remind yourself how important your vision is to you. Visualize yourself, in full color, living a fulfilling life. I want you to speak aloud this affirmation at least once a day:

> I am only one. But I am one. I can't do everything,
> but I can do something. I will influence
> and inspire my students with the life I live.

2. Find an accountability partner. It is important that you find a trustworthy partner who is not afraid to coach you along the way while giving you constructive feedback.

3. Keep a journal. This is a good general practice, but especially as you work through this book you will want to record your thoughts. Every time I instruct you to write something down, I suggest you record your responses in your journal. Provide a header with the topic or question that prompted your entry, so you will be able to find it again in the future.

4. Don't read this book straight through. Read only the chapters that address specific areas in which you would like to improve. Then read them again! Only after you've soaked up the most pertinent information should you move on to read the rest of the book.

5. Don't read just to say you read this book. Instead, stop throughout your reading to think how you can apply these ideas to your life, as both a teacher and a person. Write the ideas in your journal.

6. Use a highlighter and a pen. When you find something that makes you want to stomp your feet in agreement, mark it boldly so you can find it again later.

7. Read carefully the parts that speak to you, then re-read them, and read them over again. Mull them over and think all around them. George Bernard Shaw said, "If you teach a man anything, he will never learn." Shaw was right! Learning is not a static process but an active one. You learn by application and involvement. Passive learning doesn't stick, but what you use does!

8. Create an accountability check system for yourself to keep track of your growth in the aspects of your life you have decided are key for you. Check it daily. By doing so, you are emulating Benjamin Franklin, who at the age of twenty embarked on the pursuit of moral perfection. He developed a list of thirteen virtues, gave each a clear and short description, then proceeded to track how well he did on a chart of his own devising. While

he evaluated himself daily on all thirteen virtues, he would each week select one as his special focus.

9. Put the things that don't currently apply to you on the back burner. Remember that when a student is ready the teacher will appear. Things that are not relevant to you today may well become so in the future. When you are ready, those ideas will be there for you, waiting.

Chapter 1
Start With Why

Just a thought : Teaching is the application of your passion.

Students are drawn to teachers who are good at communicating what they believe. Your ability to make students feel like they belong, to make them feel special, safe, and not alone is part of what gives you the ability to inspire them.

I remember I had to write my philosophy of education in order to earn my undergraduate degree. It was long and filled with theories from men long dead. In all honesty, my written philosophy did not actually reflect my thoughts on why I accepted teaching as my vocation. Honestly, it wasn't until I truly gained some teaching experience that I knew my why for becoming an educator. But I am certain of one thing: if you don't know why you are an educator, you have a major problem.

German philosopher Frederick Nietzsche said, "He who has a why can endure any how." Knowing your why is an important first step in figuring out how to achieve the goals that excite you and create a life you enjoy living—versus merely surviving! This is the key. You can't win students if you are living a life you don't enjoy. Indeed, only when you know your why will you find the courage to take the risks necessary to succeed as a teacher, to stay motivated even when the test scores are down, and to move your life onto an entirely new, more challenging and more rewarding level.

While there's no one pathway for discovering your life's purpose, there are many ways to gain deeper insight into yourself and a larger perspective on just what it is that you have to offer the world.

You can only become truly accomplished at something you love. Don't make money your goal. Instead, pursue the things you love doing, and then do them so well that people can't take their eyes off of you.
— Maya Angelou

What is it that drives you? Your reason probably isn't money—at least it shouldn't be, if you're in education. There's a reason that career counselors across the world ask the same time-old question: "If money were no object, what work would you pursue?" it is an indicator of your underlying motivators.

Passion is as contagious as colds are in a kindergarten classroom. When your enthusiasm is genuine, your students will want a ticket on your happy train. The key to harnessing that passion is understanding your why. Just know as a selfless educator, you deserve a life you love, so get going and dream on.

Your why does not have to be "standards based" or "common core." Your "why" as a teacher is not to increase your students' test scores but to equip them for real life.

Life's Work Assignment

Think about what makes you happy. Write it down. How does this relate to your teaching? Okay, now write your why statement.

Your Why Statement: ____

____

____

____

____

____

____

Chapter 2
Shh! The Biggest Secret to Developing Relationships with your Students

Just a thought 🔍 : Treat your students the way you would want your administrators to treat you.

Every educator should own a profound respect for all students at all times.

Point.
Blank.
Period.

In the age of social media, it seems that the whole world converges upon an educator who has made a single bad decision. The media continue to highlight teachers who disrespect students or talk down to them. This is totally unacceptable. If, as an educator, you expect students to show you respect, you must first show them your respect for them. Model the behavior you wish to see.

Go on YouTube and search for "disrespectful teacher" or "teacher abuse." You will find a myriad examples of embarrassing and unprofessional conduct by teachers. Educators should be smart enough to know that in an age where cell phones are as prevalent as the common cold, their actions will be recorded and seen outside of the classroom.

In times of great pressure it is okay to step back and take a moment to calm yourself before you respond. Call to mind the fact that many of your students come from economic and social situations that are far from ideal. Your classroom and your school should at all times be a safe haven for all learners, as well as for you.

Each student is unique. Each is as different as a fingerprint. Practice embracing those differences. If, on the other hand, you view your students as little robots, you will be bored out of your mind. So will they.

Try this little exercise called patience. Before you say anything to your students, stop to choose your words carefully. Your tone matters as much as what you say. It isn't easy, but you must always handle interactions with your students in a positive manner. Never embarrass a student. Speak in terms of positive improvement, but do not reprimand a learner.

Remember, you were once a student yourself. Your students are going to make mistakes; it would be the height of presumption to expect them to be perfect. If you do, you are only setting yourself up for frustration, burnout and failure. Give your students enough space to learn that it's okay to be human.

There is a difference between having unrealistic expectations and high expectations. Unrealistic expectations are things beyond your students' current capacities or outside of their control. If you demand things that are beyond their capacity to handle, it can put a soul-crushing burden on your students that saps their desire – and their hope – for success.

High expectations, on the other hand, are invigorating and life-infusing, because your students instinctively understand that they are not only possible to attain, they are right, in the deepest sense. High expectations invite your students to stretch up to their full height and expand to their full capacity, living up to the expectations set before them.

Let me share with you several ways you can earn a student's respect:

- Be Consistent–Students must know what your expectations are every day.

- Be Flexible–Be sensitive to every situation and be willing to modify or even abandon your scheduled plans when necessary. Teachers who aren't flexible are setting up both themselves and their students for failure. Things happen in a classroom that are beyond anyone's control, so keep an open mind and remember your lesson plans are not set in stone.

- Be Fair–Treat every student the same in a similar situation. Providing a different set of consequences for different students for the same actions will undermine your authority.

- Laugh a little–A sense of humor can be wonderfully inviting. Students will look forward to coming to your class and learning if they know that you aren't uptight and rigid.

- Sustain a Positive Disposition–An educator with a positive attitude toward his or her students and the job in general will be highly effective. All of us have bad days, but we should still strive to remain positive, even on our worst days.

Let me share with you some ways you can avoid losing your students' respect:

- Never misuse your authority.
- Never avoid smiling and being friendly toward your students.
- Do not scream.
- Avoid adopting a consistently negative attitude.
- Do not be afraid to apologize or admit it when you've make a mistake.
- Do not discuss, gossip, or complain about other teachers in front of your students.
- Never issue vindictive threats; they are counter-productive.
- Never give control over to your students.
- Do not be hypocritical.
- Do not say anything that you would not want recorded and played back.
- Do not humiliate or berate students in an attempt to get them to behave.
- Never use sarcasm. (I still struggle with this sometimes!)
- Never use profanity. (Out loud. In your head is a safe place!)
- Do not violate a student's personal space.
- Do not limit learning to the classroom

Life's Work Assignment

Remember your best teacher. How did he or she make you feel? What did this teacher do that made you feel this way? Visualize yourself interacting with this teacher, then write down, in as much detail as possible, what you saw. Ponder how you act similarly toward your students.

Chapter 3
Show Humility

Just a thought : Humility is the solid foundation of all virtues. —Confucius

The epic downfall of an awesome teacher occurs when she falls in love with the sound of her own voice and only hears the voices of her students when they are parroting her words. Humility is the teacher's ability to sustain a realistic self-image, neither overly exalted nor as a doormat.

Humility matters. One day a student came to me at the end of class, holding a paper I had just returned, with a less-than-acceptable grade. "This is wrong," she said. "Ted answered the same way I did, and his answers weren't marked wrong, but mine were." She was obviously worried and a little afraid.

I looked and, sure enough, I had marked several questions as wrong when they had been answered correctly. While she waited, I corrected her paper and my grade book. "I apologize. I was wrong," I said as I returned her paper. "Wow! A B-plus," she smiled, no longer anxious. Then, with a brief, "Thanks!" she was off. It was a little thing, the work of a moment, but my honesty in admitting I had made a mistake, had set her world right again.

The art of teaching and learning is already complex, requiring courage on the part of all involved to facilitate students taking the kind of risks that are vital for real learning to occur. It doesn't need to be further complicated by competitive egos on the part of the teachers.

Real strength – the kind that doesn't come because one has a title that says "Educator" or "Teacher" or even "Education Reformer" – requires an almost Zen-like state where all we do emerges from a centered core that is confident enough to listen to others who hold opinions that differ from our own.

Teaching is not for the fainthearted. It takes great courage to deal with your stuff and present yourself honestly before your students. It is essential that we teachers create a solid barrier between our personal and our professionals lives. If we don't, our personal issues will eventually bleed over into the classroom and undermine our effectiveness with our students. At the same time, this provides another reason to deal with our own stuff. We owe it to ourselves, as well as to our students, to face our issues head-on.

Humility is also about stepping back and letting others do things for themselves. It includes letting your students come up with their own ideas and own them, offering space enough for them to create things you would never have thought up. It means knowing enough not to presume that you know everything.

As a teacher you are a leader, but humility must be your best friend. Humility lends tensile strength to your leadership by making you open to the opinions of others and by giving you the ability to self-reflect.

Lao-Tzu, an ancient Chinese philosopher, made a wise observation about the successful leader:

- He does things without desire for control.
- He lives without thought for private ownership.
- He gives without the wish for return.
- Because he does not claim credit for himself, he always receives credit.

Humility pervades the consciousness of the influential teacher. As a leader, your humility will enhance your influence. Students will follow you more enthusiastically when they perceive that you have worthy and selfless motives. Humility allows you to experience personal fulfillment through watching students move toward achievement.

Life's Work Assignment

What does humility mean to you? Write down your idea of humility and what it looks like as you live it out.

____

____

____

____

____

____

____

____

Chapter 4
Persuade Your Students And Foster Intellectual Curiosity

Just a thought : Foster intellectual curiosity and excitement in your class and connect content to students' current lives.

Let me tell you one thing about arguing with students: don't. Arguing with students is likely to get you the opposite of what you want, because nobody likes to lose. It pays to remember that students have minds of their own and that they are much more likely to change their minds on their own than to have an aggressive and arrogant teacher do it for them.

There is a highly underrated skill you can use to persuade your students to do what you want. It is called listening. If you actively listen to your students, if you pay sympathetic attention to them, you will begin to understand what makes them tick. Too many teachers make the mistake of relying on their title of teacher, believing that influence lies in keeping their mouths moving. Such a teacher barks a good game but over the long term will not inspire loyalty and confidence.

Have you ever been listening to someone you like and admire when they paused to ask your opinion? You couldn't help but feel happy. For that moment you were the expert. That invisible connection gave the relationship an extra layer of strength.

Listening influences others far more than speaking. Shut out your ego and listen.

Life's Work Assignment

Describe a situation in your life where careful, respectful listening made all the difference in a relationship.

Chapter 5
The Power Of Positive Thinking

Just a thought : Be cheerful. If a student is having a negative day stop the transfer of energy.

Every human is like a container of energy. This energy can be positive or negative. While you cannot control how your students treat you, you can control how you respond to them.

Positive thinking is a mental and emotional attitude that focuses on the bright side of life and expects positive results. A positive-thinking educator anticipates happiness and success and believes that all students can overcome any difficulty or obstacle. An educator with a positive attitude will encourage happy feelings. That attitude will show in your eyes as you greet your students. Your whole being will broadcast happiness, good will, and success.

Now, I know not all kids will accept your positive thinking, but you can create an environment in which it is hard for them not to. Negative thoughts create unhappy behavior and moods. When a mind is negative, toxins are released into the bloodstream causing negativity to boil over.

Whenever a negative thought enters your mind, take notice of it and replace it with a constructive idea. If the negative thought returns, replace it again with a positive thought. It is as if there are two pictures set in front of you; you choose to regard one of them and disregard the other. Persistence in choosing will eventually train your mind to think positively and to ignore those negative thoughts. It is an issue of mind over matter. Just imagine how consistent positive thinking could infect your whole classroom!

Life's Work Assignment

Create an affirmation for yourself and your students. Affirmations are positive statements that describe a desired situation, event, habit or goal. When these positive statements are repeated often, preferably spoken aloud, they engrave themselves on our beautiful subconscious mind, clearing the way for them to become reality.

____

____

____

____

____

____

____

____

Chapter 6
Teach With Grace

Just a thought : Understanding grace
is what gives you peace in your classroom.

As an educator, it is easy to think that you are automatically in authority because of your position. Well, let me share a secret with you: Authority is an inner quality. Influential teachers understand that authority does not come from a title or a degree.

Here are eight traits of grace-filled teaching:

1. Emphasizing principles rather than rules. Principles change mindsets and hearts; rules modify behavior. Any student can adjust his or her behavior for a class period in order to adhere to a given structure. Lives are truly changed, however, through transformation rather than tradition. When we focus on principles, we teach students wisdom and lay a foundation for their own future good choices.

2. Valuing students. It is easy to view students as a means to success in our classrooms. If our students feel cared for and valued

for who they are, not merely for what they do, we will have their hearts and their loyalty. This involves listening to our students and finding ways to serve them; our motivation is a simple desire to see them succeed.

3. Pushing toward excellence but leaving room shortcomings. As gracious teachers, we know our own weaknesses and failures. This gives us the ability to push students towards success while allowing them to make mistakes. After all, our own best teachers allowed us to learn some of our greatest lessons through failure. No one wants to work for a teacher who demands an impossible level of perfection.

4. Promoting unity while allowing different opinions. One of the leading traits of insecure teachers is over-controlling. Insecure teachers hurt students. Gracious teachers recognize the need to surround themselves with other strong teachers. They value differing strengths and ideas, both among their peers and in their students.

5. Praising in public; chastising in private. Be realistic. Gracious teaching cannot avoid confrontation, but do so one-on-one and in private.

6. Permit students to experience the consequences of their actions. True grace realizes lessons are often learned by experiencing the results of a bad decision and learning from them. Grace does not remove consequences or attempt to protect people from their bad decisions. Grace trains.

7. Believing the best. We must trust our students and colleagues, doing away with judgment, a critical spirit and a suspicious attitude. This value allows us to truly free people to do their work. Only in so doing can we avoid micro-management.

8. Willing to be insulted. Grace filled teachers sometimes are accused of being taken advantage of. You were a student once and you know students naturally look for loopholes or ways to work the system. You can use this to your advantage, creating loopholes that will actually benefit your students, when they walk through them.

Life's Work Assignment

Do you teach with grace? What are areas in which you could improve?

____

____

____

____

____

____

____

____

Chapter 7
Yes-Yes

Just a thought : Get the student
to say "yes" at the beginning.

Do not begin class by discussing the things you will not tolerate. Instead, begin by emphasizing, and keep on emphasizing, the things that you believe are true. Point out that you, collectively, are working toward the same end result. Your methods may differ, but your purpose is always the same.

Do not provide a chance for your students to tell you "no." An effective teacher provides a way for students to say "yes" from the outset.

Life's Work Assignment

How can you practice giving your students the "yes" option?

____

____

____

____

____

Chapter 8

Stop Giving Orders.
Start Making Suggestions.

Just a thought 🔍 : The best teachers spend seven
times (seven is my favorite number) asking questions
rather than telling students what to do.

Think about your former teachers. Chances are your first visual image will be of a teacher standing in front of a classroom giving orders.

If you think a teacher's primary role is to be a classroom COO—Chief Order Officer—you are super-wrong! Telling isn't teaching. It is better to offer your students the opportunity to work things out for themselves. Don't you think your students would learn more from your suggestions than from your handouts?

This simple strategy will save your students' pride and give them a feeling of importance and accountability. Your suggestions promote cooperation instead of provoking rebellious conflict. Asking open-ended questions can spark creativity and fuel curiosity.

Students will be more likely to follow when they are included in the exploration. This shifts your role to that of a CEO – Chief Empowerment Officer! By your questions you can empower your students to pursue learning for themselves.

Life's Work Assignment

What exactly is your questions-to-orders ratio?

Chapter 9
Shift Happens

Just a thought : Stay conscious
and prepare them for the future.

Shift doesn't just happen once nor does it happen in a vacuum. It's happening all the time. How will you manage the shift in your classrooms? The answer is simple: stay conscious and aware. Understand that you have to be a futuristic thinker and facilitator. Imagine your desired classroom into existence.

We spend a great deal of time discussing ways to help students master the curriculum. We plan, build, and differentiate instruction to meet the diverse learning styles and needs of our students. We do whatever is in our power to ensure that students are assessment-ready. But are they ready for the future?

I am calling for us to rethink our role as teachers from that of givers of information to facilitators of learning. Shouldn't we teach our students to be positive thinkers? Shouldn't we teach our students to be atypical thinkers, to be life-long learners, to grow, change, and adapt? Shouldn't we be equipping our kids with the skills and talents they need to work in diverse environments—perhaps in environments that do not yet exist? Shouldn't we be preparing them for a world that does not yet exist?

Shouldn't we encourage students to adopt a positive relationship with information and learning and to sharpen their digital literacy? Shouldn't we spend more time planning to facilitate students in building meaningful connections and gaining access to resources and tools to solve problems? Yep, we're talking problem based learning. Shouldn't we be creating self-directed learners? Shouldn't we face the hard truth that textbooks and lectures are outdated and no longer useful?

Yes, shift is happening. Either you are going to get on the boat or be left behind.

Life's Work Assignment

Shift your thinking about the classroom.

- **Begin by taking time to reflect on the way you are thinking about your classroom.** Ask yourself: what thoughts do I have about my classroom and my students? Write down every thought that comes to mind.

- **Examine each item on your list and start asking questions. Ask yourself: how do I know this thought is true?** What if it wasn't true for me? Where did this thought come from? Are these thoughts what I really believe or are they what I was raised to believe? And ultimately, does this thought still serve me, the classroom as a whole, and the individual students I want to serve?

- **Make a list of new thoughts.** Write down what you would like to experience in your classroom. What would you need to believe in order to experience it? Start by asking "what ifs". Instead of immediately assuming something can't happen, counter-attack negative thoughts with "What if I could?" "What if it could happen easily?" "What if it was like__________?" [Fill in your desired experience]

- **Pay attention to how each thought makes you feel.** Does a thought make you feel empowered or do you feel powerless? Does it make you feel lighter or heavier? Thoughts that feel good and create positive emotions are life-giving thoughts for you.

- **Start focusing on what you do want to experience, not on what you don't want.** Imagine your classroom just as you would like it to be. Visualize it for five minutes or so each day. Pay attention to any limiting thoughts that arise and respond with, "Thank you, but no thank you" to them. Replace negative thoughts with thoughts that support what you are aiming for.

- **Take action.** Every little step toward what you do want matters. Pay attention to your guidance, how the universe leads and opportunities follow. But don't wait for the universe to perform a miracle for you; make what opportunities you can.

Chapter 10
Manipulation Versus Inspiration

Just a thought : Inspire them.

There are two ways to influence a student's behavior. You can either manipulate the behavior or you can inspire it. The choice is yours. Yes, manipulation. I bet you have done this many times in your life. Parents do it all the time with their kids. "If you are good at the doctor's, I will take you to McDonalds"—a highly effective tactic employed by parents to obtain the behavior they want from their kids.

Manipulation is all around us—from politics to common business practices. Typical political manipulations include "Vote for me and I will reduce your student loans"; or "Vote for me; I will work hard for equality." Typical retail manipulations include using inspirational messages, dropping the price, implying the fear of a shortage or even using personalized advertisements.

Just because manipulation works doesn't make it right. Manipulating students has become the new norm, creating systematic pressure. This, my friends, is the classic carrot-and-stick approach.

According to Wikipedia, the carrot-and-stick approach

> is an idiom that refers to a policy of offering a combination of rewards and punishment to induce behavior. It is named in reference to a cart driver dangling a carrot in front of a mule and holding a stick behind it. The mule would move towards the carrot because it wants the reward of food, while also moving away from the stick behind it to avoid its pain, thus drawing the cart.

The carrot-and-stick approach does not work well in the classroom with today's learners. According to thought leader Daniel Pink, there are seven deadly flaws to the carrot-and-stick approach.

It can:

- extinguish intrinsic motivation
- diminish performance
- crush creativity
- crowd out good behavior
- encourage cheating, shortcuts, and unethical behavior
- become addictive
- foster short-term thinking instead of the pursuit of long-term objectives

Your mission, if you choose to accept it, is to replace all temptations to manipulate with inspiration. Conspire to inspire your students.

Life's Work Assignment

Let's inspire our students to embrace intrinsic motivations for learning. Write down five manipulating tactics you have used in your class. Revise them to inspire your students.

1.____

2.____

3.____

4.____

5.____

Chapter 11
Life Is A Pitch: Change It Up

To win a student : Give a new pitch.

We have all had the experience, both as teachers and learners, of drifting off part-way through a class or a professional development workshop. In such a situation we can benefit from the tactics of a baseball pitcher. One relatively non-intrusive tactic you can employ to counteract the attention gap is to utilize a "change-up" in class. By throwing the ball at different speeds the pitcher keeps the batter off-balance.

The concept can work as well in the classroom as on the baseball diamond. For example, by mixing brief periods of application into your teaching, changing the form of instructional media, or altering your delivery speed (your talking speed, volume, and inflections), you can help students stay alert and actively learning for an entire class. Moreover, change-ups afford students multiple opportunities to wrestle with difficult concepts ultimately enhancing student learning. Keep in mind that change-ups need not consume large amounts of class time but can be seamlessly integrated into a class.

Life's Work Assignment

Think of a few ways you can weave change-ups into your class.

Chapter 12
Improvisation

To win a student : Keep yourself free of judgment.

When we think of improv, we think of Saturday Night Live, or comedy clubs, right? Improv can occur in education as well.

According to Dictionary.com, improvisation is defined as "the art or act of improvising, or of composing, uttering, executing, or arranging anything without previous preparation." Is it possible to improvise in the classroom? Yes, it is, if you have an open mind. Use these six educational steps to building improvisation into the classroom:

- Let go of your agenda. Be open to anything.
- Listen in order to discern what the students may need next.
- Build on discerned needs as you respond.
- You can't fail if you remember to listen.
- Make your students look brilliant. Set them up for successful learning.
- Keep moving forward. Don't stop teaching.

The first rule of improvisation is "yes, and," meaning that anyone's contribution to a group discussion is freely accepted without judgment. Improv is built around the Four Cs of "Creativity, Critical thinking, Collaboration and Communication." These are four essential skills if we want our students to become good global learners. Once students have been persuaded to abandon their fear of making mistakes, they will work to build trust in your classroom, making it open to the possibilities and challenges of risk- taking.

Improvisation not only sharpens communication and public speaking skills, it also stimulates quick thinking and fast engagement with ideas. On a deeper level, improvisation gradually removes mental barriers that block creative thinking—our internal editor that crosses out every word before it appears on a page—by rewarding spontaneous, intuitive responses. Improv is one of the few opportunities students have to truly create, to have a voice that isn't prescribed for them. This form of communication is based on open observation and collaboration and is not bound by the constraints of a lesson plan.

Life's Work Assignment

Research two improvisational exercises you will implement in your classroom. Once you have tried them out, reflect on your students' responses.

Chapter 13
Serve

Just a thought 🔍 : Just serve.

One of my favorite places in the world is Chick-fil-A. This is not because I want to eat more chicken but because of the servant leadership it models. There are at least five lessons you can learn from Chick-fil-A's business model, each of which can be implemented in your classroom.

Lesson 1 - Ambiance: The next time you go to Chick-fil-A, check out the little things they do to make their restaurants warm and attractive. They have flowers on the tables, photos of employees, inspirational quotes on the walls, paintings from community children, and so forth. Everywhere you look in one of their stores you'll find something that makes you smile. There is not a dull corner.

Take Action: Make your classroom warm and open. Celebrate your students by posting their work. Add photos of your family and their families.

Lesson 2 - They know what they're great at. Many businesses try to be a jack of all trades, which ends up with them mastering nothing but failure. That's why Chick-fil-A will never have a burger on their menu. Why? Because they don't care. They know they'll never be the best at beef but they sure as heck excel at creating a culture around the chicken sandwich. Wow, what a lesson this is for teachers out there who lack any identity or clear sense of individual greatness!

Take Action: As a teacher, identify your strengths. Understand them and stay in your own lane, making the most of what is yours. Don't ignore your weaknesses but let your strengths, not your weaknesses, dictate your instruction.

Lesson 3 - They're clean. Sanitation and cleanliness have become a lost art in the fast food industry. Counter to this trend, Chick-fil-A's restaurants, as well as their restrooms, are always clean. I don't know about you, but I'll pay more for clean any day of the week.
Take Action: Keep your classroom clean and your desk organized. Model what you want from your learners.

Lesson 4 - Happy employees and great service: It's unbelievable how many great employees this company has. While I was eating my meal the other day, an employee approached with a big smile on his face to ask if I'd like a refill on my drink. For a fast food company, this – both the smile and the service – is utterly unheard of.

Take Action: Choose to be happy. If you are not happy, your students will not be happy.

Lesson 5 - The food is actually good. Ah yes, let's not forget this other oft-overlooked trait of fast food restaurants—great food. Almost everybody likes Chick-fil-A. Nothing on their menu is of poor quality. They're proud of their food—they have every right to be!

Application: Offer lessons of quality. Throw out the copy paper. No more worksheets. Offer students authentic projects and problem-based learning activities.

Life's Work Assignment

If possible, stroll into a Chick-fil-A restaurant for lunch. Just sit, absorb the goodness, and observe how they serve.

Answer these questions:

1. If a student chooses to learn from you, will his or her life improve?

____

____

____

2. When your interaction with a student is over, will the world be a better place?

____

____

____

Chapter 14
Build Moral Character

Just a thought 🔍 : Be the moral character you wish to see.

As we seek to prepare our learners with global skills for career success, Warren Buffet reminds us what makes great employees:

In looking for people to hire, look for three qualities: integrity, intelligence, and energy. And if they don't have the first one, the other two will kill you.

As educators, we are charged with building moral character into our learners. Here are thirteen ways to build moral character:

1. **Surround your students with moral examples.** Make sure you are a positive, affirming role model and surround your students with people of high character.

2. **Stress service!** Students don't learn how to be kind from a textbook but from doing kind deeds. Encourage your students to lend a hand so they will understand the power of "doing good."

3. **Teach virtue as an action, not just as a noun.** The best way to teach students any virtue is not through our lectures but through

our example.

4. **Stress WE not ME.** Teach your students the value of collaboration.

5. **Halt your biases.** Get in touch with your own prejudices and be willing to change them so your students won't pick them up from you.

6. **Find an unjust cause to support.** Look for opportunities in your neighborhood or community to get involved in making the world a better place. There is no more powerful way to boost students' moral intelligence than to get them personally involved in an issue of injustice and then encourage them to take a stand; they will learn that they can make a difference in the world.

7. **Be a moral example.** Become the living textbook of morality that you want your child to copy.

8. **Don't assume!** Take time to describe and show students how to be kind—or fair, just, honest, patient, frugal, etc. Never assume they already have absorbed a virtue.

9. **Encourage them to choose to delay gratification.** Gradually stretch your students' ability to control their impulses. Help them learn to wait.

10. **Aim for internal motivation.** Refrain from always giving tangible rewards for your students' efforts. Instead, let them develop their own internal reward system.

11. Take a deep breath! To teach students self-control, you must show students your self-control. Be a living example of restraint.

12. Acknowledge goodness. Catch a student acting morally, describe what he or she did right, and explain why you appreciate it.

13. Show – don't just tell – your students about moral behavior. To teach students excellent behavior, you must model what the virtue looks like in action. Reduce the sermons; increase the visuals. Students learn more by seeing an example in context, than by hearing or reading about it.

Life's Work Assignment

Note five ways you can model moral character to your students.

1.____
2.____
3.____
4.____
5.____

Chapter 15

Create A Balanced Classroom, Not A Busy Classroom

Just a thought : Do we forget that we are human beings, not human doings?

Did you know that being busy is a disease? This disease of being busy– and let's call it what it is: a dis-ease, a state in which we are never at ease – is spiritually destructive. It destroys our health and our sense of wellbeing as well as the health and wellbeing of our students. This dis-ease saps your ability to be fully present and to live in the moment.

"The unexamined life is a life not worth living."
-Socrates

How are we supposed to live, to learn, to examine, to be, to become, or to be fully human when we are so busy?

How did we create an educational system in which we have more and more to do with less and less time for leisure, less time for reflection, less time for community, less time to just . . . be?

Life's Work Assignment

Find a time every day where you can just sit quietly by yourself for fifteen minutes. Practice, in the words of Eric Fromm, "the art of being."

Chapter 16

Teach What You Never Learned In School

Just a thought : Life is a process.

Life Lesson 1: Life is not fair!

Life Lesson 2: Smile more! It changes peoples' perspectives.

Life Lesson 3: Everyone has weaknesses. Focus more on your strengths.

Life Lesson 4: Rejection is not the end of the world; it is merely internal fuel for your next attempt.

Life Lesson 5: Give more; you will find that you receive more, in the end.

Life's Work Assignment

If someone had taught you that life would be a process, would you have changed your perspective on life?

Chapter 17

Teach Your Students How To Have A Growth Mindset

To win a student : Teach your students that the brain is malleable or "plastic."

Dr. Carol Dweck, a professor of Psychology at Stanford University, found that students who believe they can develop their basic abilities and improve themselves have greater motivation and higher achievement than those who see their abilities as fixed and unchangeable.

Step 1: Help students identify their "fixed and unchangeable voices."

Teach your students that as they approach an obstacle, they might hear a voice saying things like: "Are you sure you can do this? Maybe you don't have the talent." "What if you fail—you'll be a failure."

"People will laugh at you for thinking you're that great." "Why even try? Protect yourself and keep your self-respect."

As the student hesitates, she might then hear that voice becoming even more critical and harsh: "This would have been a easy if you really had talent." "You see, I told you it was a risk. Now you've gone and shown the world how lame you are." "It's not too late to back out, make excuses, and regain your dignity."

Let your students know that as they face criticism, they might hear internal defensive statements like: "It's not my fault; it was his fault." They might feel themselves growing angry at the person giving them feedback. "Who do you think you are? I'll put you in your place." Even with specific, constructive feedback, they might hear negative messages between the words, such as, "I'm really disappointed in you. I thought you were capable, but now I see you're not."

Step 2: Help them see that their attitude is a choice.

How students interpret setbacks, challenges, and constructive criticism is their decision. They can view those messages through the lens of a rigid mindset, as signs that their talents are fixed or that they will always lack ability.

On the other hand, students can view the same messages through the lens of a growth mindset. This way of thinking allows them to interpret setbacks as encouragement to ramp up their efforts, stretch themselves, and expand their abilities. The choice is up to them.

Step 3: Change their language, change their lives

Teach your students that as they approach a challenge they can counter everything the fixed mindset throws at them. Help them create the following dialogues:

The **fixed mindset** says, "Maybe you don't have the talent. Are you sure you can do it?"

The **growth mindset** answers, "I'm not really sure I can do it now, but I have faith that I can learn with personal effort over time."

The **fixed mindset** says, “What if you fail? Folks will laugh at you and you’ll be a big failure.”

The **growth mindset** answers, “Most successful people experience multiple failures on the way to success. Everything will be okay. I would rather fail than live with the regret of not trying.”

The **fixed mindset** says, “You can protect yourself from embarrassment if you don’t try.”

The **growth mindset** answers, “ If I don’t try, I automatically fail. How epic is that?”

Life’s Work Assignment

Practice developing your own growth mindset. Observe your language for the next 24 hours.

Chapter 18
Practice Patience

Just a thought : Understand that they have to practice patience with you too.

"Trees that are slow to grow bear the best fruit."
— Molière

Teaching with passion and love requires patient praise. Too often praise is an afterthought. Think about it. Of course, when you grade a student's paper you write "good job" or "keep up the good work." But for praise to be truly effective it should be spoken. You are already patient enough to observe what your students have done; your patience also allows you to wait for the perfect moment to deliver words of praise.

Patient praise should be "clean;" it should exist without any conditions. If you are trying to compliment a student by saying, "I really appreciated the work you did on your science today," and then tag on, "but you need to finish your math assignment," the student will likely only remember the part following the "but."

On another note, praise without specific feedback can be worse than no praise at all. Unless the learner hears praise that he can attach to something he has done, it can leave him feeling left out, as if the praise is not for him at all, but for someone else more worthy.

In difficult situations, great tact and patience are called for. Please understand, we don't have to accept poor performance, but we must be patient in our response to poor performance. Sometimes no response at all is sufficient to motivate a student to improve.

It is also important that your praise be legitimate. False praise can destroy your credibility entirely. Students can sniff out deception and hypocrisy a mile away, so don't even try to fake it.

Praise more than you admonish. Expert opinion varies, but the general consensus is that you should praise a student at least four times for every single instance when you offer correction.

When it is necessary to admonish your students, do so in private. Private admonishment allows the student to save face, protecting one's dignity. My mantra is: praise in public, correct in private.

When you deliver admonishment, get to the point. Be specific. Describe exactly where the student erred, and then provide specific guidance to put the student back on track. Following your admonishment, pay attention to your student's behavior and, as soon as you see the correct actions, affirm them with praise and specific feedback.

Life's Work Assignment

Think about a time when someone praised you for something you did well. What made the praise "stick?" How did it make you feel?

____

____

____

Chapter 19
Write 'Em Up!

Just a thought : Write positive notes.

No, I do not mean you should write an office referral.

I used to write notes to my whole class. I didn't have the time to handwrite notes for each of my students, but I personalized my class notes to make everyone feel special. This is an invitation to transform the awful injunction "write 'em up" into something students can look forward to. It is an act of kindness.

Kindness, in the context of teaching with love, begins with you. Writing each student a simple note is a form of active, loving encouragement, an act of kindness. Unfortunately, this is done all too infrequently. How do you think a note of encouragement will impact your students? Being kind starts with you and is the key to teaching with love.

Student enthusiasm will never rise higher than your own. You can make any student's day better. Every time you interact with a student, you can make his or her day better—or worse! Before each class, reflect on the previous day and think about what you want to reinforce. This puts you in a new position, giving you a different title. You are now the CEO (Chief Encouragement Officer) of your class.

Life's Work Assignment

Write 'em up: Write an encouraging note to your class as a whole or to your students, individually.

Chapter 20

Enhance Your Belief System

Just a thought : Change your perception of your students.

To be or not to be is not the question. The question that matters is, "How do teachers' beliefs impact students' academic performance?" Researchers have validated what, to most teachers, is an obvious answer. A recent study confirmed that student performance improves when teachers believe their students are gifted intellectually.

Bob Pianta, Dean of the Curry School of Education at the University of Virginia, conducted the following study: He assessed two groups of teachers regarding their beliefs. One group then received personal coaching and intensive behavioral training while a second group completed a traditional course on effective teaching.

After the training, the teachers were recorded on video in their classrooms and evaluated. Dean Pianta then reassessed the teachers' beliefs. His study concluded that the teachers' beliefs shifted much more dramatically as a result of the behavioral training, thus confirming that behavior, rather than understanding, influences belief.

A teacher's belief system wields significant influence on student behavior. Therefore, as teachers, we must embrace that by our beliefs we can stimulate right behavior in our students.

Life's Work Assignment

Write down your beliefs about your students.

Chapter 21
Make Them Comfortable

Just a thought : Make a safe place.

Once our students see our beliefs in action, hopefully they will be intrigued enough to seek to better understand us, to learn what motivates our thoughts and our behaviors. As a result, our students will develop better communication skills and enjoy even more enriching learning experiences.

Envision your students feeling their way across a scary suspension bridge of belief. Students don't want to venture down an unknown path unless they can anticipate their destination. What do you do and say to keep your students moving forward? The process is as delicate as helping a toddler learn to walk.

You do not shout at them or shove them. You do not want them to become fearful. Instead you respect and affirm their feelings. You provide guidance and freedom. You expose them to familiar and consistent signals that will allow them to grow confident that they are in a safe place.

Making your students comfortable is about keeping their minds fully engaged through rich associations while appeasing their skeptical thinking minds.

Life's Work Assignment

How did your good teachers make you feel comfortable? What did they do?

Chapter 22
You Don't Have To Like Your Students

Just a thought : Act like you like them.

I am going to be honest with you. I acknowledge that over the past ten years, I have had some students that I wish I could pay to stay home. After talking to many educators, I have learned that we all have had a few such students. I am here to tell you that you don't have to like all your students—you just have to act as if you did. The rationale is simple: if you act like you don't like your students, it doesn't matter if you really do. But if you act like you like them, then whether you really do like them or not becomes irrelevant.

Pause and reflect on the teachers you most loved as a child. Do you think they liked some students more than others? Of course they did! But ask yourself this: How did they treat the students they liked the least? The best teachers treat the ones they like least just like all the other students. Whether they like a student or not, they act as if they do.

Life's Work Assignment

Think of one student you really don't like. Write five positive things about that student.

1.____
2.____
3.____
4.____
5.____

Chapter 23
Stop Trying To Fix Their Weaknesses

Just a thought 🔍 : Embrace their
weaknesses and cultivate their strengths.

The main reason students lack the motivation to live up to their potential is because too much focus is placed on improving their weaknesses rather than developing their talents and strengths. A talent is a natural skill or aptitude. Strengths are the result of developing one's talents. This can include responsibility, positivity, creativity or other strengths that may not be easily measured on a standardized test, but are strengths nonetheless. Unfortunately, our educational system does not focus on a student's natural abilities; instead, it is driven by low test scores and substandard performance. The one thing that would inspire and motivate our students to grow and thrive is being ignored, in our focus on weaknesses.

Let's stop trying to fix our students' weaknesses and spend more time cultivating their strengths. Teaching your students to acknowledge and leverage their strengths does not mean you are teaching them to ignore their weaknesses. Instead, you are teaching them to use their strengths to overcome their weaknesses. Studies now show that assisting students to build on their strengths yields major improvements in their overall grades.

Life's Work Assignment

Think of a time when you taught a highly successful lesson. What strengths did you use to accomplish this? How did you use your strengths to shore up your weaknesses?

Chapter 24
Become A Reflective Teacher

Just a thought : Be reflective.

It takes consistency to be the best teacher you possibly can. In order to sustain your enthusiasm you must focus on your own professional and personal development. The most significant indicator of student success is the personal development of the teacher. In order to grow into an epic teacher, you must give yourself time outside the classroom to interact with other positive thinkers.

Identify those individuals who influenced you to become a teacher. I would bet there were two or three teachers who discovered and nurtured your hidden gems of talent. When you identify and define the excellent qualities those teachers exhibited while you were their student, you begin to define the roots of your own teaching excellence.

Life's Work Assignment

Write down five qualities of the individuals who influenced you to become a teacher.

1.____

2.____

3.____

4.____

5.____

Chapter 25
Use Technology

Just a thought : Integrate technology into your classroom.

When you go to the hardware store to buy a hammer, you don't actually want a hammer, you want a hole. They don't sell holes at the hardware store, but they do sell hammers, which represent the technology you use to make holes. We must not lose sight that computer technology is a tool, just like the hammer. The tool of technology is most appropriately used to address specific educational concerns.

In kindergarten, I was introduced to the Apple II computer with its floppy disks. My kindergarten teacher, Mrs. Pam Smith, herded us into the library and seated us in front of a large screen. Then the librarian demonstrated the computer and its use. She even showed us a game," The Oregon Trail"—the "Candy Crush" of that era. "The Oregon Trail" was the most popular computer game of my generation. It was simple, informative and interactive. Honestly, I cannot tell you how many times I got my wagon stuck in the mud or how many classmates I killed off with cholera or malaria.

For us, the computer was simply the tool that allowed us to get things done – in this case, completing "The Oregon Trail". It gave us a welcome break from the classroom. Mastery of computer skills was one way to show we were advancing beyond our classmates.

In middle school, my mom bought our first home computer—well kinda-sorta. She bought a used Tandy from a yard sale, which I used just for typing. She even purchased a Smith Corona word processor so I could print out my assignments.

It wasn't until I was in junior high that we were able to hook up to the Internet. Our initial dial-up connection was snail-like compared to the instantaneous broadband speeds available today. It ran so sluggishly that I used to remark that my Gateway computer was always in the slow lane. However, we were still able to surf the web.

I think these experiences helped to shape my understanding of how technology can fit into the classroom. Our students learn by doing, not by being forced to study a meaningless list.

Technology provides tools for active learning, but they are only tools—not the solution. Integrating technology into our pedagogy stimulates us to reflect on our role as teachers, to think about moving away from the ways things have always been done toward fresh imagining of ways things might be done.

A question reflective educators ask themselves:

How can I make this current lesson more relevant, applied, connected, practical, collaborative, and multidisciplinary?

Computing technology can augment and support your teaching and can facilitate student learning in three important ways:

1. It can broaden the scope of learning beyond the narrow physical boundaries of the classroom.

2. It can broaden accessibility to, and engagement with, genuine

content and real-world information.

3. It can exponentially expand the ways students can demonstrate and organize what they have learned.

Life's Work Assignment

Visit www.techtechteach.com to explore ways you can integrate interactive technology into your classroom.

Chapter 26
The Winning Formula

Just a thought : Implement the winning formula,
P+A+O+A=Winning students.

Preparation: Personal growth is extremely important for the prepared teacher. By consistently improving and enhancing your knowledge, skills, relationships and access to resources, you will be ready to win students.

Arnold Palmer said in the February 2009 issue of Success magazine, "It's a funny thing; the more I practice, the luckier I get." The more you prepare, the more students you will win.

Attitude: You are not the only teacher in the world, so stop whining about little Johnny who doesn't want to listen or Suzy who comes to school ill-prepared. Countless teachers have faced greater disadvantages and obstacles than you ever will, yet they succeed because they view life as full of opportunities, instead of difficulties.

Opportunity: Look for teachable moments for your students and for yourself. Many opportunities await you.

Accountability: Enlist the help of a mentor or peer teacher with whom you can review your successes and struggles and gain wisdom for the future.

Life's Work Assignment

Write at least one affirmation statement that outlines how you intend employ the P+A+O+A formula to win your students.

____

____

____

____

____

____

____

____

____

Chapter 27
Be The Light

Just a thought : Be the light in their darkness.

One of the finest teachers the world has seen in the last century was Mother Teresa. This short, frail, and humble nun chose to make it her life's work to care for people who were unable to care for themselves: the homeless, the outcasts and the forgotten. Over the course of her life, she worked tirelessly to promote this singular cause.

Committed to bringing hope to the hopeless, healing to the hurt and dignity to individuals on their deathbeds, she was a light in the lives of those who were experiencing their darkest moments. Isn't that your role as a teacher, too? You are charged with teaching the lame, enhancing the vision of the blind, and loving the unloved and unlovable.

Life's Work Assignment

Write your reflective response to the following quotes:

1. "There is a crack in everything. That's how the light gets in.
— Leonard Cohen

___

2. "Darkness cannot drive out darkness: only light can do that. Hate cannot drive out hate: only love can do that."
— Martin Luther King Jr.

Chapter 28
Stay Cool As A Cucumber

Way to win student 🔍 : Take time to be patient.

The unfortunate truth is that far too many educators are so eager to force a strategy to work that they lose perspective and balance in the classroom. Let's consider Herman Melville's Moby Dick. This tale provides a great example of the importance of being able to relax in the middle of turmoil.

In this story there is a horrifying, turbulent scene in which a small whaleboat crosses the roiling ocean in pursuit of Moby Dick, the great white whale. The sailors were straining every muscle in their bodies and expending all of their energy in their efforts to master the sea in their small vessel. Yet in this wooden boat, there was one man who did absolutely nothing. He did not hold an oar or break a sweat. This man was poised, calm, and waiting. Then we read this sentence: "To insure the greatest efficiency of the dart, the harpooners of this world must start to their feet from out of idleness, and not from out of toil."

As teachers, much of our work consists of waiting, poised and alert, to take advantage of teachable moments when they arise. It is up to us to steadily resist the temptation to become embroiled in the chaotic details of administering a learning experience. Your challenge, if you choose to accept it, is to keep at least a small part of yourself separate, so that you can maintain a semblance of objectivity in the midst of the ever-shifting landscape that is your classroom

Life's Work Assignment

Describe a time when your ability to retain objectivity helped you guide your classroom through a difficult experience.

Chapter 29
Show Them You Care

Just a thought Understand that students don't care until they know how much you care.

It was Mark Twain who said, "One learns peoples through the heart, not the eyes or the intellect."

Students do not care how many degrees you have or how many years you have taught. They only care about how much you care about them. Too often teachers and students seem to hold an adversarial relationship. Instead, our task is to be like the little girl when she was confronted by five mean girls, any of whom could have smashed in her face. As with many of us, she was not equipped to fight that battle, but she was qualified to think.

The little girl took two steps back and drew a line in the mud with the toe of her sandal. She then stared the ringleader of the bully crew in the eye and said, "Now you just step across the line if you are bad." As you may have guessed, the mean girl took her up on her offer and crossed the line. The little girl then said, "Now we are both on the same side"

If we are going to be successful and inspire our students, we must remember that teachers and students are on the same side. It is up to us to take the initiative to draw students – many of whom do not yet see this truth – to our side, connecting with them where they are, and loving them into the community of learners

Anyone can teach. However, it is not until there is warm love in a teacher's heart that the results are great. Love's purpose is to pour into others, to teach, to be loyal both to Truth and to our students, and to contribute richness to their lives.

Life's Work Assignment

Describe a situation in which your students didn't respond until they could see how much you cared about them. What did you do to get this truth across to them?

Chapter 30
A Recipe For Inspiring Students

Just a thought : Be loyal to your students.

1. Invest time in classroom activities that bring the highest return for your instructional time investment. Results are the only reason for any classroom activity.

2. Fulfilling a responsibility is a good reason for work; discipline is the method.

3. Acknowledge and accept your own weaknesses.

4. Teach for progress, not for perfection.

5. Show honest and sincere appreciation.

6. Develop a purpose for teaching that is bigger than your ego.

7. Never criticize, condemn or complain.

8. Always show students gratitude and humility.

Life's Work Assignment

Which tips from this recipe list are part of your life?

Chapter 31
Seven Winning Principles

Just a thought : Remember how
you wanted to feel as a student.

1. Model the behavior and the attitudes you want your students to have.

2. Remember, a warm smile is the most powerful tool we have as educators.

3. Only make requests, not demands!

4. Always be respectful of your students' time; give performance feedback in a timely manner.

5. Ask questions you already know the answer to, in order to learn the students' perspective. Then you can lead the students further down the path of discovery.

6. Meet your students where they are.

7. Listening is one of the most neglected skills in education. The

teacher who listens controls the final outcome. Encourage your students to talk and consciously remove any barriers from your epic listening skills. You must be silent to listen. Note: both words are formed from the same letters. S-i-l-e-n-t and L-i-s-t-e-n.

Life's Work Assignment

Reread these seven principles once a day for five days.

Chapter 32
Don't Worry. Be Happy.

Just a thought : Behind a group
of happy students is a happy teacher.

The title of this chapter is not a cliché! Harvard Professor and author of The Happiness Advantage, Shawn Achor, said, "Happiness fuels success, not the other way around." When we are in a positive frame of mind, our brains become more engaged, creative, motivated, energetic, resilient and productive in our work.

A happy teacher means a happy classroom.

Achor also stated that the three best predictors of happiness are our perception of stress, our optimism, and our social connections.

Here are five activities you and your students can do daily.

Activity 1 –Gratitude

You: Write down three new things that you are grateful for each day.
Your students: Write three things they are grateful that they learned.

Activity 2 – Journal

You: Write for two minutes about a positive experience you've had recently.
Your students: Write about a positive experience in your class.

Activity 3 – Exercise

You: Engage in fifteen minutes of mindful cardiovascular activity.

Your students: Do three jumping jacks during class transitions.

Activity 4 – Meditate

You: Watch your breath go in and out for two minutes each day.

Your students: Pay attention to your breathing while you complete a class assignment.

Activity 5 – Perform Random Acts of Kindness

You: Write a positive sticky note thanking or complimenting someone you admire in your school.

Your students: Write a positive note to a classmate.

Life's Work Assignment

Make a list of five people you will engage in a conscious act of kindness.

1. ____________________
2. ____________________
3. ____________________
4. ____________________
5. ____________________

Chapter 33

The 8 Essential Qualities Of A Teacher Who Inspires

Just a thought : If you can become the learner you want to be on the inside, you will be able to become the teacher you want to be on the on the outside.

Students will want to follow you. When that happens, you'll be able to tackle anything in your classroom. Here are some personal characteristics that will impact your students as you develop them:

Character: Stand on your beliefs and don't let yourself be easily swayed from them.

Charisma: Focus more on making others feel good about themselves than on making them feel good about you.

Commitment: This quality separates doers from dreamers. To the teacher, it's all that and more because everyone you teach is depending on you.

Communication: Simplify your message. It's not as important what you say, as how you say it. Communicate your care for your students.

Exemplify Truth: Let your life match what you say is important. Believe what you say and say what you believe.

Competence: Work your skills.

Problem Solving: you can't let your problems be a problem. Teachers with good problem-solving abilities demonstrate five qualities:

- They anticipate problems.
- They accept the current reality.
- They begin with the end in mind.
- They focus on one thing at a time.
- They endure; they keep on working until the problem is solved.

Self-Discipline: The first person you teach is you. Teachability: To keep teaching, keep learning

Life's Work Assignment

Which of these essential qualities are yours?

____

____

____

____

____

____

Chapter 34
Give Your Students Two "A"s

Just a thought : Anyone can have these.

I bet you cringed as you read that. Give your students two A's? The two A's I want you to give your students are for excellence in Attitude and Appearance.

Infuse your students with an attitude of confidence in their ability to learn. Greatness and excellence grow from a foundational attitude of self-confidence. You want your students to believe they can succeed in the classroom.

As a teacher your success in the classroom seems to stem from your undying confidence in and commitment to your own abilities. If you project an attitude of confidence in your students' ability to learn, they will see your undying commitment and begin to believe in their own skills.

Secondly, appearance matters. Let your external greatness reek of internal excellence. Appearance is simply a manifestation of your attitude.

Life's Work Assignment

Do a mirror check. How do your physical appearance and your facial expressions communicate a spirit of excellence?

Chapter 35
Get A Mentor

Just a thought 🔍 : Apply to your students what you have learned from your mentor.

Success rarely occurs in a vacuum. The most successful teachers are those who have built positive relationships that grow into personal and professional learning communities.

There is nothing new under the sun, so there is no need to hide your challenges as a teacher. When you are willing to submit your fears to others and admit your uncertainties regarding how to handle a situation, you will often find affirmation and fresh solutions to the problem through your interaction with other people.

Ecclesiastes 4:9-12 summarizes the importance of mentorship and a professional learning community:

> "Two are better than one, because they have a good return for their labor:
> If either of them falls down, one can help the other up.
> But pity anyone who falls and has no one to help them up. Also, if two lie down together, they will keep warm.
> But how can one keep warm alone?
> Though one may be overpowered, two can defend

themselves. A cord of three strands is not quickly broken."

Can you name a person who has made a positive and enduring impact on your personal or professional life, someone worthy of being called your mentor?

Let's start by listing questions to ask your mentor. Remember to be a learner, listening more than you speak. Here are a few questions to get you started:

- What is the best decision you ever made?
- How did you know it was the best?

At a critical moment, successful teachers make decisions that may fly under the radar as a "best" decision. As you discuss your choices with your mentor, you will see how good decisions can enhance your influence on your students for years to come.

- What is the worst decision you ever made? How did you know it was the worst?
- What made it your worst decision and what would you do differently if you had known better? (Listen carefully to these answers so you can avoid making the same mistake.)
- What is one thing you wish you had known when you started teaching? (Let your mentor's hindsight be your foresight; this question can significantly shorten your learning curve.)
- When you face a disappointment, how do you handle it?

Successful teachers are often those who can see the good even when things go badly.

Those who succeed are typically those most willing to take

risks and ask for forgiveness later.

- A Japanese proverb says, "Fall seven times. Stand up eight." What strategies do you employ, from an emotional and mental standpoint, to keep getting back up?
- What is the wisest step you think I could take in my career right now?
- What is the best advice you can offer me right now?

A mentor relationship is a two-way street. To make it work, you should bring something to the party. Offer your time, your strengths, and your skills in exchange for the time and effort your mentor expends in order to help you.

Life's Work Assignment

As you have opportunity, begin to ask these questions of your mentor.

Chapter 36
Exercise Your Ability To Ignore

Just a thought : Understand that everything does not require feedback.

Great teachers have an unbelievable ability to ignore certain things. This does not mean that they are oblivious to what is taking place, neither does it mean that they have the patience of Job—although that might help! Instead, it shows their mastery of the experiences that arise as part of the daily life in the school setting. These teachers know how easily one or two students can kill the flow of learning. Epic teachers know when to go with the flow and when to put their foot down. They know how to address minor disturbances without disrupting the learning of other students. They know how to pick their battles.

Teachers must know how to attend to trouble and when to look away. We often must make these decisions on the fly. Great teachers have learned from experience; they know which situations demand immediate attention and which moments are truly teachable.

An epic teacher has the ability to pay attention to students, recognizing and praising their achievements, while overlooking minor errors. This is a delicate balancing act, but the awesome teacher has mastered this essential skill.

Life's Work Assignment

Reflect on a behavioral situation you might have chosen to ignore, but didn't. If you had ignored the student's behavior, how might the class have been different, for better or for worse?

____

____

____

____

____

____

Chapter 37
Plan With A Purpose

Just a thought :
Create a purpose-driven classroom

Clarify your objectives as a classroom teacher by using purpose-driven planning. One hallmark of awesome teachers is that very little happens in their classrooms a without purpose. Epic teachers have a purpose-driven plan for everything they do. If things do not work out the way they envisioned, they reflect on what they could have done differently and then shift their plans accordingly.

Inexperienced teachers, on the other hand, can move through their days more randomly. It may appear as if they don't want to have a plan because then they would have to take responsibility for whatever happens. If things do not work out as well as they had hoped, they would have to look for a way out or find someone else to blame instead of themselves.

You weren't put in the classroom to be remembered; you were put there to prepare your students for the future. So remember, your students' will to win is worthless if you do not have the will to prepare the way for them.

Life's Work Assignment

Ask yourself, "Am I implementing purpose-driven plans that give me direction for today and increase my students' potential for tomorrow?"

Chapter 38

Top Inspirational Quotes For Teachers

"Education . . . is painful, continual and difficult work to be done in kindness, by watching, by warning . . . by praise, but above all —by example." — John Ruskin

"The job of an educator is to teach students to see the vitality in themselves." — Joseph Campbell

"There are two kinds of teachers: the kind that fills you with so much quail shot that you can't move, and the kind that just gives you a little prod behind and you jump to the skies." — Robert Frost

"The greatest sign of success for a teacher . . . is to be able to say, 'The children are now working as if I did not exist.'" — Maria Montessori

"Education is not to reform students or amuse them or to make them

expert technicians. It is to unsettle their minds, widen their horizons, inflame their intellects, teach them to think straight, if possible."
— Robert M. Hutchins

"It is important that students bring a certain ragamuffin, barefoot irreverence to their studies; they are not here to worship what is known, but to question it. " — Jacob Bronowski

"Teaching kids to count is fine, but teaching them what counts is best." — Bob Talber

"Tell me and I forget. Teach me and I remember. Involve me and I learn." — Benjamin Franklin

"Everybody is a genius. But if you judge a fish by its ability to climb a tree it will live its whole life believing that it is stupid."
— Anonymous

"The important thing in life is not the triumph but the struggle."
— Pierre de Coubertin

"Creativity is especially expressed in the ability to make connections, to make associations, to turn things around and express them in a new way." —Tim Hansen

"Always to see the general in the particular is the very foundation of genius." — Arthur Schopenhauer

"Stay committed to your decisions; but stay flexible in your approach." —Tony Robbins

"They may forget what you said but they will never forget how you made them feel." — Carol Buchner

"Treat people as if they were what they ought to be and you help them become what they are capable of becoming." – Goethe

"Every truth has four corners: as a teacher I give you one corner, and it is for you to find the other three." – Confucius

"Good teaching is more a giving of right questions than a giving of right answers." — Josef Albers

"Read not to contradict and confute, nor to believe and take for granted... but to weigh and consider."— Francis Bacon

"Let the potential artist in our children come to life that they may surmount industrial monotonies and pressures."
— Barbara Morgan

"Come forth into the light of things, let nature be your teacher."
— William Wordsworth

The best leader speaks little.
He never speaks carelessly.
He works without self interest
and leaves no trace.
When the work is accomplished,
the people say: "Amazing:
we did it all by ourselves."
— Lao-tzu